PRESENT

TRUTH

PRAYER, PRAISE
& PROPHECY

KATHY HANSON

Acknowledgments

To God be the glory!

This book is dedicated to some very famous people! I mean, like VERY FAMOUS PEOPLE! But you may not know them. See, they may not be known to you, but their names are very well known in HEAVEN.

To those that have spoken into my life: Fran and Ed Kreiss, Jean Huggins, Elizabeth Edelen, Maggie Gore, Laurel and Tracy Abell, Tyler Miller, Debbie Blaise, Theresa Capel, and Debbie Moore.

To those who held me up the past few years when I was unable to stand on my own, Amie LaBrozzi, Jenn Patil, Leisa Glotfelty, Charlene Ragland, Carolyn Cook, Stacy Blanton, Revive Now, and my Friday morning warriors Kristie Narango and Michelle Richardson.

To my husband Steve, and my daughters Savannah Faith and Cassandra Joy, I love you most!

Table of Contents

2 Peter 1:12 KJV

"Wherefore I will not be negligent to put you always in remembrance of these things, though ye know them, and be established in the <u>present truth</u>."

About the Book

Please don't let the title "Present Truth" scare you off. I am not claiming a "new doctrine" or "new revelation" just the opposite. I am referring to Peter's Epistle and the ancient paths of New Testament truth.

I have included numerous scripture references to support what I share. I believe we as Christians have left the present truth of Peter's day and exchanged it for our own experience. We create doctrine from that experience and not what we read from the Holy Word.

The Bible is quite clear about doctrine, but we often trade what the Scriptures say for man's theology. That should never be. We should read the Word of God and BELIEVE IT! I hope this inspires you to do both.

Also, this book has been covered in prayer. Prayer and fasting have been offered up for those who choose to read it.

1

"And the peace of God, which surpasses all comprehension, will guard your hearts and your minds in Christ Jesus." Philippians 4:7

Introduction

A funny thing happened to me on the way to church. It sounds like an opening to a joke, but is actually a true story. An important truth and a message for today but not the least bit funny. As a matter of fact, it couldn't be more serious. But first, there is something I want to share about even writing this book.

Before I was saved and in my 20's, I was in a bar one evening with my sister-in-law Karen in Fells Point, Baltimore, MD. This was back in the eighties, and there was a fortuneteller in this bar. I had my fortune told to me that night that I would write a book. I told Miss Fortune Teller then, and I believed until the beginning of writing this introduction, that it would never happen.

I know, I know, a fortune teller? God can and will use anything or anyone/thing to get us a message. Why not a fortune teller? It is like a prophet to the lost. And I was very, very lost. I wasn't saved so why wouldn't I get my fortune told in a bar. Why do I/we expect unsaved people to act any other way than unsaved?

The miracle of the evening isn't the telling of the fortune. It is that decades later (shhh, we won't discuss

3

my age), I remember something so insignificant from something I didn't believe in then and didn't want. I am not a writer. I don't even journal for heavens' sake!

Something just as funny happened just a few months ago. I was at my friends Ed and Fran's house and Ed looked me right in the eyes during prayer and said: "You need to write a book."

I jokingly said, "I think I might!"

It wasn't until I was on a flight home from South Lake, Texas after attending a "Power and Love" Conference and visiting my daughter and some dear friends that I began to believe that maybe, just maybe, I WAS supposed to write a book. I had been reading the book "Giants Will Fall' by Dutch Sheets and I saw through the book my authority, obligation and most importantly the last three chapters I *saw* on prayer, praise and prophecy.

I know, I have an incredibly quick mind....talk about not getting hints...

Perhaps, the Lord *was* speaking to me to write a book.

Now, I agree with you that getting your advice from a fortune teller is *a really, really, bad idea.* I would never seek one out today nor do I recommend it ~ever!
At the time, I didn't know any better and had not committed my life to Christ.

Did God use the fortune teller for good? It certainly

isn't unheard of in the Bible. Even Paul had a witch following him around proclaiming the truth. Granted, the reasoning behind it was dark, but the truth itself was being proclaimed.

However, Paul didn't want the truth coming from a witch. He didn't want the newly saved to turn to the dark side (sounds a little like Star Wars) to get their information. It is what happened in the Garden of Eden! So, Paul shut it down.

And neither should we want our information coming from the darkness either because as in the Garden of Eden, it can have slight distortions and errors that lead us astray- lead us to sin, and even to death. God has given us gifts through the Holy Spirit that leads, guides, instructs, and much, much, more.

So why a book on prayer, praise, and prophecy? As I said, a funny thing happened to me on the way to church.

I was riding down the road on my way to church one Sunday morning. I live in Pennsylvania where the roads are windy and beautiful and curvy, and you can get lost in worship music. I always get lost in the music…

It wasn't a long ride to church, but I do remember just worshiping when I heard in my spirit very loudly and distinctly:

Prayer, Praise, and Prophecy!

Prayer, Praise, and Prophecy!

Prayer, Praise, and Prophecy!

I kept repeating it to myself out loud in the car. But then (if you know me, it won't strike you as strange) I started to rearrange the words the Lord had given me.

I was thinking maybe praise, prayer, and prophecy. Yup, that's how I would do it. Let's start with praise, like in a church service, followed by prayer leading into prophecy. Certainly a better order, as if I knew better than God.

But don't we all at times try to rearrange things and think we know better than God. The Bible is full of such examples so I find myself in good company, albeit wrong. Certainly, God didn't mean.... (fill in your blank), *just like in the Garden...*

I continued my trip to church and had an enjoyable time that day. I later came home and headed for my computer, not something that I usually do on Sunday afternoons. I was going through my email and came across an advertisement for Revive Israel, a group of Israelis in Jerusalem that meet to preach Jesus as Messiah. Not knowing who they were or how it got into my inbox, I opened it for this two-minute ad. They were talking about the Messianic Jewish congregation that they have in Jerusalem and how their goal is to bring together 'the one new man-the Jew and Gentile.' They explained that they do this every morning through, wait for it…. prayer, praise, and prophecy!!!

I nearly fell out of my chair! I couldn't believe what I just saw and heard. I played it again and again and again. Could this be real? I tried to explain this to my daughters. I explained what happened to me in the car that morning and how I heard the same prophetic words from this advertisement from this group I did not know. They didn't seem to be nearly as impressed or overwhelmed as I was. They merely asked if I was okay, because, honestly, I wasn't acting ok.

Well, at least I knew one thing for sure: God had the right order. It certainly was prayer, praise, and prophecy!

I couldn't even speak to my daughters because I was so overwhelmed at this God coincidence. I shared this same story with a few people, and I did the only thing I knew to do. I began to meet with some people for, you guessed it, prayer, praise, and prophecy. It was a small group that we called Revive NOW! We met on Tuesday evenings at my home, and God did some amazing things.

Through a series of events, I got to know some new people who became great friends, reunite with some old friends, and prayed, praised, and prophesied with some girlfriends.

It was met with some resistance from people inside the church, because it was not understood, and I had some wild accusations come my way. (Satan doesn't like it when you use God's gifts).

And that is why I am writing this booklet.

By the way, if God gives you an idea or a prompting, GO WITH IT! Don't let others deter you or keep you from pursuing where God is leading. If you are assuming wrongly, you will know soon enough. Trust me, God will have you and will lead you.

The modern-day church should be more on board with prayer, praise, and prophecy. Many already are, and because of some outstanding ministries, the numbers are growing. However, many are not.

We should embrace the supernatural because God is supernatural and its part of Gods Kingdom and His methodologies. It is how Jesus, the MAN, grew his disciples and followers by showing His power from His Father through the Holy Spirit.

Please understand, some tell us in the Church that healing is not for today. If Jesus, who is God, used these gifts as a man to profess His Kingdom, certainly we need them. We follow Him and His example. And if the newly established church needed them, how could Christianity possibly survive in the end times when "all hell" is breaking out on earth, without them.

Question? Does the church seem powerless to you? I mean, for the most part, the church has relinquished her authority and thus her power to the government and the world. Could it be because we relinquished our power, at least in part, that this is the result of believing that the some gifts are not for today? Are we like Thomas? We need to see it to believe it. God says believe and you will see.

There are many things that we as the Church disagree on. This should not be one of them.

I'm not hoping for division, although I know, when addressing this topic, it will come. I am praying through my obedience, and in my sharing what God told me to share, that this booklet will compel like-minded people to get together and work for His Kingdom through His Word and His Way!

One last thing. I know that some of you reading this book may disagree with some of my interpretations of the Bible. So, know this, I believe the Bible. I believe what it says and how it's presented, and I reverence the Word! What you need to know is translations can change the understanding and meaning of words and concepts. Because of the many changes in history we also need to look at context. Context is key (Thank you, Joseph Prince!)

I do quite a bit of work exploring into the original languages of the Bible which are Hebrew, Greek, and

Aramaic. One of the greatest examples that I'd like to cite in the Bible of how interpretation can fail us is our understanding of the account of Jesus teaching the Sermon on the Mount.

Jesus says in Matthew 5:48,

> **"Therefore you are to be perfect**
> **as your Heavenly Father is perfect."**

While I agree our Heavenly Father is perfect, let's take a look at the word perfect as it refers to *us*.

That word in the New Testament is teleios and means: *finished – that which has reached its end, term limit; hence, complete, full, wanting in nothing.*

Figuratively, in a moral sense, of persons.

Jesus saying "that ye may be perfect" means that you may keep yourself "unspotted from the world." Or in a relative sense:

The teleios is one who has attained a moral maturity, the goal for which it was intended, namely, to be obedient to Christ.

Saying we are to be mature brings a whole new understanding to the statement than telling us to be perfect. A new believer is at a different maturity level than a seasoned saint.

Just as parents we have different expectations of our children as they age and mature, so does our heavenly

Father. We don't expect a newborn to feed themselves, or change their clothes but we do expect it from a school-aged child. We also don't expect an elementary school child to drive a car or to care for themselves when we are away, but we do from an older teen.

God is no different. As we grow in Him - we mature. God expects us to grow in Him through knowledge, wisdom, and understanding! Again, context is *KEY*!

A person who is newly saved and reads this particular Bible passage could come away with a completely different interpretation than someone who has an understanding of the Greek translation of- be perfect. They may think, "I try and try and try, but I fail. Often. Every day. Why try? I might as well give up." Satan will bring those thoughts.

And may I ask how many of you know people who left the Church? Or perhaps you know people who take the opposite road and misuse grace as an "everything goes" approach because we are forgiven, Jesus paid the price, and perfection is unachievable. Let's be honest; there is only One on earth who ever achieved perfection, and His name is JESUS.

That can and has led to failure, frustration, quitting, trying, leaving, and backsliding. None of which are part of God's plan. Yes, He may use them but...

The Bible, although very complex and intricate in some ways, is very literal and easy for even children to understand. And after all, aren't we told to come to God as little children to receive?

God calls himself Father, ABBA, because he wants that kind of relationship with us. HE WANTS US TO KNOW HIM AND KNOW HIS WORD AND HIS WAYS! The Bible is not a secret to His children. It is a love manual. And when we pray before we read and we ask the Holy Spirit to help, we can expect to have understanding.

John 14:26 states:

> *"But the Helper, the Holy Spirit,*
> *whom the Father will send in My name,*
> *He will teach you all things,*
> *and will bring to your remembrance*
> *all that I said to you."*

For those who disagree, it will be most likely because they believe in the cessation of the gifts of the Spirit.

Again, let's put this in context.

1 Corinthians 13:8-13 says,

> *"Love never fails;*
> *but if there are gifts of prophecy,*
> *they will be done away;*
> *if there are tongues, they will cease;*
> *if there is knowledge, it will be done away.*

For we know in part and we prophesy in part;
but when the perfect comes,
the partial will be done away.
When I was a child, I used to speak like a child,
think like a child, reason like a child;
When I became a man,
I did away with childish things.
For now we see in a mirror dimly,
but then face to face;
now I know in part, then I will know fully
just as I also have been fully known.
But now faith, hope, love, abide
but the greatest of these is love.

We see again how maturity plays into not only our behavior but our understanding. Paul, in all of his understanding, says he still only sees in part. Some have concluded that this scripture suggested when the Bible was canonized, or compiled in the third century, that is exactly what Paul was referring to when he says "**when the perfect comes**," meaning the canonization of Scripture.

However, Paul does not stop there. He says when we are face to face, actually meaning eye to eye contact. That will not happen until we go to Heaven or the rapture. That will be our face to face encounter with God Himself.

None of us fully know now, thus the importance of

supernatural gifts *and* even with the gifting, we still only know in part like Paul.

I believe, if the early Church needed the gifts of the Spirit, so do we! The End-Time church won't be fighting the Roman Empire but the Antichrist and all the powers of evil and influence allowed by our modern world.

Twelve men turned the world upside down because they were entirely sold out to Jesus Christ. I'm convinced that if we want to do the same today, we need to be sold out to Jesus, and filled with His power and gifts the same as the Apostles were.

Satan will stop us any way he can. He targets us as individuals, as families, as churches, as regions, states and nations. He will stop at nothing to go after the Bride of Christ. But, Christ conquered Satan at the cross.

Colossians 2:15 states,

> "When He (Jesus) had disarmed the rulers and
> authorities,
> He made a public display of them,
> having triumphed over them through Him."

We win! Are we not seated in Heavenly places? That is what God says in His Word.

Kings rule from their thrones. God rules from His throne. We rule from our position in Christ as representatives and ambassadors. We are the righteousness of God in Christ Jesus!

For our victory to be secure we need two things to happen. We need unity in Christ and a love walk! That is living totally sold out and powered up to serve our Savior.

PART 1

PRAYER

Jeremiah 29:12

"Then you will call upon Me and come
and pray to Me,
and I will listen to you!"

1 John 5:15

"And if we know that He hears us in
whatever we ask,
we know that we have the requests
which we have asked from Him."

Prayer may be the single most underutilized weapon we have.

Wait... Prayer is a weapon?

Many of us are unaware of the real power of prayer. We have been taught in some expressions, that it is a repetition of words. It is not a "now I lay me down to sleep" before I go to bed, so I wake up in the morning thing. Prayer is not only communicating with God above, but it is also ruling, commanding and declaring *all* the things God has laid on our hearts from His Word.

We should be taught to be careful with our tongues because Proverbs 18:21 states,

> **"Death and life are in the power of the tongue, and those who love it will eat the fruit."**

We truly don't take that to heart! If we knew what prayer is, what it does, and how effective it is, we certainly would do it more often! After all, Paul instructs us to pray without ceasing!

1 Thessalonians 5:17 says,

> **"Pray without ceasing."**

Pray without ceasing? How can we do that?

The Greek word for without ceasing (*adialeiptos*) does not mean nonstop – It means continuously or recurring. So we are to bring our prayers and petitions before the Lord continuously.

The good news is Our Father never tires of hearing from His children. I know as a Mom I never tire of hearing from my kids. I often feel like I don't see or hear from them enough. Are you getting the picture?

Paul is trying to tell us God doesn't hear from us enough. He never slumbers or sleeps and WANTS to hear from us. He yearns to hear from us, just as we yearn to hear from our children.

My daughter lives far away, and at times I physically ache to hold her or talk with her, especially if she is sick or upset. I miss her, very much like God misses hearing from us. Sometimes relating to God may feel like a long distance relationship. But, here's the thing, God is never far away. He may "feel" far away, or seem "deaf" to our concerns, but He loves us more than we can imagine, more than we love our own children. So much so, He comes to live inside us when we follow the instructions given to us by Paul.

Romans 10:9-10 declares,

> That if you confess with your mouth
> Jesus as Lord,
> and believe in your heart
> that God raised him from the dead
> you will be saved;

for with the heart a person believes,
resulting in righteousness,
and with the mouth he confesses,
resulting in salvation.

God paid a BIG price to have a relationship with us – it cost Him HIS SON! How many of you would give up your child for another? Unfathomable! How rich is God's love for us?

Still, we don't pray. We need to make prayer a priority like the early Church. They knew prayer was a priority because JESUS MADE PRAYER A PRIORITY! Jesus is our SAVIOR! He is not only an excellent example to follow, but He is our source for everything!

Colossians 1:16-17 tells us,

"For by Him all things were created, both in the heavens and on earth, visible and invisible, whether thrones or dominions or rulers or authorities, all things have been created through Him and for Him. He is before all things, and in Him, all things hold together."

We live in a time where we have more modern conveniences than at any other time in history, yet our time seems to escape us. It can and will continue until we get serious about the assignments God gives us and our need for prayer. I know it's hard, but, I assure you, nothing is more important.

And then there are times, hard times when we can't seem

to pray as we should, as we need. It is those times of trials and tribulations when we have been crushed by death or loss, that despite our desires, we can't seem to pray. There were times I've wanted to, but I was in pain physically or emotionally and didn't have the words or the strength.

Just two years ago, I buried my mom. I can tell you there are parts of your heart and your mind and your body that feels like recovery will never happen. You can feel yourself, especially on the very onset of the loss, as though you may never get over the sorrow. But, we need faith and hope in God above and in what the Scripture says about having resurrection life in Christ; we are not without help. We are not without hope. The faithfulness of God will never leave us, nor will it leave us in a place of pain. Pain is never desired, but it is sometimes necessary.

Just like a woman in labor, it leads to greater things. Women do not want labor pains, but they are willing to pay the price of pain for their reward is their child. Just like Christ's example of suffering unto death for the price of us, His Bride. He did not want the cup of wrath that was poured out on Him, but He was willing to buy us back and gift us to His father.

And just as pain is experienced in childbirth, so is the pain we can experience in other areas of our lives. I know the pain of infertility. For ten years my husband and I tried to have children, and we were unable. We had numerous miscarriages and after many failed pregnancies, surgeries, medications, and treatments, and still no children, my doctor told me that we would never realize our dream of becoming parents.

BUT, I had a promise! I believed God's promise that one day we would have an inheritance.

A Promise Received

Ten years from the time of my first loss, I was genuinely struggling.

"Should we try again?"

"What about my promise?"

"Where was God?"

"Was I wrong?"

"Should we try again?"

"Should I be satisfied with my job and serve God as a working woman?"

The thing is, before I was saved, I never considered having kids. I said as much. I remember telling my mother that I was more than a baby machine and I could have a purpose in my life without children. I was very happy with my life, and many in my circle of friends were not having children, so it was a good fit. We were DINK's (double income no kids) and as a working woman, I didn't feel the need. I enjoyed my life and I enjoyed my work, and besides I'd had several failed relationships, and thought I might never marry.

But, I did meet a man who I fell in love with, married, and, ultimately wanted to have children. But the real heart change came when I met another man.

If you are not familiar with Romans 8:28, you need to be. It is a promise that every single son and daughter of God needs to know and cling to, especially during times of crisis.

It reads:

> **"And we know that God causes all things
> to work together for good to those who love God,
> to those who are called according
> to His purpose."**

I had a great job before I met my husband. I worked with some really fun people and life was a blast, but it was a reckless lifestyle for sure.

Then came a bombshell. I lost my job due to downsizing of my department. All of the sudden I was a stressed out single woman living alone.

Luckily, I found another job rather quickly, even though it was less money. The day before I was to start this new job, there was a fire in my house, so I arrived at work with my clothes smelling like smoke. I was a complete wreck. I stood before my new boss explaining why I smelled like smoke and burst into tears. Needless to say, I wasn't making a great impression. Things just were not off to a good start.

But things got better and I settled in. I loved my job and my co-workers, and I was doing well in this new environment. By the way, it is also where I met my husband! Struggling through all the change and trauma, losing contact with my old work friends, starting a new job, I met some great people. As God would have it, I met two people that would change my life.

 One close co-worker and good friend of mine, Tracy, introduced me to Laurel, his girlfriend. She was a Christian. I mean - for real. Not just a churchgoer. I knew many, and in fact, I was one of them. She was different from any other "Christians" I knew. I went to Catholic School and Mass every week, but I had never known another that had the kind of relationship with God that she had. I mean, who knew that was possible...

The most important thing about my relationship with Laurel, was not my relationship with Laurel; it was that she introduced me to Jesus. I remember to this day sitting on her bed and listening to what I now know is the Gospel and wanting the kind of relationship with God that she had. If it was real, I wanted it.

My best decision ever! She even introduced me to prayer and speaking in tongues.

Not only that, Laurel showed me how beautiful motherhood could be. Not only did I admire her mothering skills, but I wanted to incorporate them into my life, and my desire for children just grew and grew.

I found out just how much I wanted children when we were told we would never have any. Unfortunately, getting pregnant wasn't the problem. Keeping the baby once I was pregnant was. It didn't seem possible.

In fact, the doctors said I was perfectly healthy, my husband was perfectly healthy, but together we were incapable of having and carrying children. But, I prayed. And I prayed. And I prayed with every believer that I came in contact with. I had people I didn't know praying. But all was silent from Heaven until one day when I was sitting on the front porch of the home that we'd purchased in Pennsylvania and I was reading my Bible. Suddenly, I just knew in my spirit the Lord was reminding me of a dream I had.

That dream happened after my first miscarriage. In the dream, I was in the doctor's office, and he told me that I was pregnant and that this baby would be fine. Sitting there on my front porch that day I clung to that promise from God believing with all of my heart that I heard from the Lord. It wasn't an audible voice, but it was an explosion inside of my spirit that I just knew was true. I held onto that promise.

Years went by and I had many more miscarriages. My faith began to wane. I could no longer pray for the promise of children. I was tired. I was broken. And I was done. At this point in my life, I thought the only way that I would ever even try to get pregnant again would be if an angel came and stood before me and told me that I was going to have a baby. You know, like an angel did with Mary! And I meant it! I didn't believe we would ever try again.

It was at this time that I went to a women's conference and was introduced to prophetic prayer. That conference changed everything.

Three different women who I did not know, nor had I ever met, prayed for me and told me that I was going to be a mother - but not just a mother in the physical. I was also going to be a spiritual mother of many.

Needless to say, I was overwhelmed and once again had a mustard seed of faith. It was shortly after I came home from that weekend retreat that I got a call from a dear friend, Charlotte.

She was like a mother to me, and she was beyond excited! She was telling me I had to watch the 700 Club that day because Charlotte heard a word of knowledge on the show about a woman who was infertile and how the Lord was going to answer her prayer and give her a baby! She said she claimed it for me and instructed me to watch it later that day and claim it for myself.

I did watch the 700 Club that day, and I got down on my knees, and that mustard seed of faith grew into a tree. Not only did I wind up having a child, but God wanted that story to be known, because my husband, my daughter Savannah Faith, and I had the privilege of being on the 700 Club and telling our story of God's faithfulness and ANSWERED PRAYER.

Not only did I have a chance to tell my testimony, but while we were filming that program, I was pregnant with my second child, Cassandra Joy!

In total, I had nine miscarriages. I had seven miscarriages before my first daughter, Savannah Faith, was born and two miscarriages after my second daughter, Cassandra Joy, was born. What a difficult and long journey, but blessings are worth it! At times we need to trust. Our ways are not His ways, but His ways and timing are perfect!

So, from my earliest days as a Christian, God's Word and prayer have been an essential part of my life and my Christian walk. I want it to be a part of yours as well. But more importantly, God wants it for you. You have to remember that when we pray we have an audience with the King- and not an earthly king, but The Heavenly King, who is The Almighty.

Another important aspect of prayer is the power of our words. Just recently the Lord convicted me of speaking curses over myself. The Lord allowed me to hear the words that I had spoken. With my own mouth, I had cursed myself.

I shared my story of infertility with you because part of that story is me CURSING myself with no children. Remember the above verse?

Proverbs 18:21
"Death and life are in the power of the tongue, and those who love it will eat the fruit."

We are told God spoke the world into existence. He breathed life into Adam. Our words, as well as our actions, have power and consequences.

The Bible is quite clear. Our words are powerful. When we are tempted to come out of agreement with God, we need to think of the consequences of our words. Are we in agreement with what we just spoke or do we want a different outcome? All of His promises are yes and amen.

God still speaks and things change. His Apostles spoke healing and resurrection. We are to do the same. Be careful little mouth what you say. May we never agree with our enemy.

But why the wait or maybe the seemingly answer of no from God? Well, we may never know on this side of eternity, but let me say some of the very things we want could destroy us. It could lead us to places we never intended on going, and yes, even those GOOD things we ask for may not be so good after all. And delays may not be our desire, but maybe they are for the benefit of others around us who are not ready for that next great move of God.

Whereas we think and function in a nuclear fashion, God moves systemically from outside of time and for the greater good. He saves us individually, but His plans are eternal and perfect.

Tongues

I can't neglect the topic of tongues. In my opinion, tongues are wildly misunderstood as a gift. You can always tell the importance of a gift by how strongly the opposition is or the misuse of it. I believe it to be a very powerful tool and feel tongues should definitely be in our prayer toolbox.

So, of course, Satan wants to dismantle this prized and cherished tool. I see tongues to be one of the most divisive things within the Christian community today.

In fact, so is prophecy, which will come later. That is the very reason for this book. I hope in love is to dispel some of the problems that we've faced in the past as the Church, and hopefully to bring understanding and unity to the body.

First and foremost I'd like to say, *nowhere in Scripture does it say that to obtain salvation you must speak in tongues nor is it proof of your salvation.*

We should never beat up on people because they don't speak in tongues. Want to turn someone off from the spiritual gifts? Tell them if they don't speak in tongues that they are not saved! Satan wins!

Likewise, it does also say in scripture *not to forbid it!*

Both teachings violate the Word of God and result in disunity, misunderstanding, bad doctrine, and poor mentoring, not to mention hardship and strife within the Church.

Faith in Jesus Christ alone is the only way to obtain our salvation and belief in His finished work on the cross. Believing that His blood was shed for our sins and Jesus is our propitiation so that we can stand before God righteously, is what is necessary. No other qualifications needed - not tongues, not anything - just Christ alone.

If we want Biblical accuracy about tongues, Paul wrote to the Corinthians about him speaking in tongues *more than anyone else.* Paul wrote this to the New Testament believers, and Paul was an incredible witness, Master Teacher, and Evangelist to many in his time. Why would we not want to follow in Paul's footsteps and use exactly what he used to accomplish what he accomplished?

Let us look at the one Scripture that some say speaks to the cessation of the gifts and why they think they are no longer available for today.

In 1 Corinthians 13, we have the beautiful love chapter which we frequently hear at many Christian weddings.

When we get to verse 8, Paul inspired writes:

"Love never fails;
But if there are gifts of prophecy,
they will be done away;
if there are tongues,
they will cease;
if there is knowledge,
it will be done away.
For we know in part
and we prophesy in part;
but when the perfect comes,
the partial will be done away.
When I was a child,
I used to speak like a child,
Think like a child,
reason like a child;
when I became a man,
I did away with childish things
For now we see in a mirror dimly,
but then face to face;
now I know in part,
but then I will know fully

just as I am fully known.
But now faith, hope, love,
abide these three;
but the greatest of these is love."

The understanding by some theologians and pastors of today is that the perfect seems to have come with the canonization of the Bible back in the AD 300's. Their understanding is that before the canonization of Scripture we only knew in part because the Holy Word was not compiled yet and now we have the perfect book which is the Holy Scriptures. They believe the gifts are no longer available or needed. I agree that the Scriptures are Holy and they are perfect in their instruction and are inexhaustible.

However, Paul writes that now we see in a mirror dimly but *then face-to-face.* That face to face proclamation by Paul is actually translated as "looking into someone's eyes."

It is an eye to eye contact with God, not a compiling of the Word. This eye to eye contact happens when believers pass from this world and go to be with the Lord or the Rapture occurs, whichever comes first. When we are face to face with our Lord, we won't need prophesy or tongues or the gift of knowledge. We will be face-to-face with Jesus Christ, and He is the Spirit of Prophecy. We won't need tongues because our new language will be heavenly. (Some believe that tongues is our Heavenly language) and we will be face to face with the Giver of all knowledge.

If we as a church teach and claim that prophecy and tongues are no longer in existence, then what do we do with knowledge that is also listed in the same passage? Are we going to throw away the knowledge that is given to us as well? I have seen some act as if knowledge is done away with.

Consider this. I recently saw a sermon by Pastor Robert Morris. He was teaching from the Gospel of Mark where Jesus sent out the twelve giving them the authority to preach the Gospel, cast out demons, and anoint the sick and heal them.

Pastor Robert made an excellent point. We are three part beings- spirit, soul, and body. The command that Jesus gave addresses the needs of *every part of our being*!

Preaching the Gospel is life to our Spirit and brings us into relationship with God. If we cast out demons that torment our soul, (which is our mind, will, and emotions) we become free to follow Christ and live our lives unencumbered by the enemy who wants to inflict mental pain, distracts us from our calling, and keep us from living life as God intended us to live. And lastly, God provides a way to have physical health and wholeness through the healing of our sick bodies. Jesus taught us that He cares about every part of us, not just our spirit. If the Church only focuses on salvation and doesn't consider healing or deliverance, we fail in 2/3 of our commission! May it not be so!

Scriptural misinterpretations have believers not fully using the gifts sent by Jesus through the Holy Spirit for the Church. This is not only a benefit for the Church, but a sign for the lost as well. And this leaves the body weak and lame. Not using the supernatural to combat evil, which is supernatural, is a poor war plan and may explain why we are seemingly losing the battle. And I want to add that I know people who are spiritually sensitive that "know and feel things" that think they are crazy or possessed because the church doesn't explain to them that they can "hear from God".

God is clear in His Word; His sheep "hear His VOICE!"

We need all the gifts: see Romans 12: 6-8, 1 Corinthians 12: 8-10, 1 Peter 4: 11. They have been given and not using them is insulting to the giver of the gifts.
Also, I believe some of the confusion comes from a misunderstanding of tongues. There is the gift of tongues which allows communication in other known languages as we see in Acts Chapter 2 on the day of Pentecost.

This use of tongues, given by the Holy Spirit, was for those in the Upper Room to communicate and educate those travelers from different parts of the world who were in Jerusalem for Pentecost. These tongues used at this time where known languages. These languages are listed in Acts Chapter 2.

While this use of tongues may not seem as widespread today, I believe we may see a resurgence of this use in the end times. As a matter of fact, Perry Stone, a well-known Evangelist, tells of his Uncle who lived in West Virginia and did not go to school past the third grade yet when he was filled with the Holy Spirit spoke in many different languages and could and would witness to the many Immigrants that worked in the coal mines of West Virginia. He could speak and witness to them in their native tongue. What a great use of tongues and why it is still needed today.

A broader use of tongues is found in 1 Corinthians 14.

Pursue love,
yet desire earnestly spiritual gifts,
but especially that you may prophesy.
For one who speaks in a tongue
does not speak to men but to God;
for no one understands,
but in his spirit he speaks mysteries.
But the one who prophesies speaks to men
for edification and consolation.
One who speaks in a tongue edifies himself;
but the one who prophesies edifies the church.
Now I wish that you all spoke in tongues,
but even more that you would prophesy;
and greater is one who prophesies than one who speaks
in tongues, unless he interprets,

so that the church may receive edifying.

Paul says "one who speaks in tongues *speaks not to men but to God."* That is the unknown prayer language of tongues. Some believe it is God's language and that it is a Heavenly language. Paul also references praying in tongues in Ephesians Chapter 6 when he talks about the armor of God. This is again, why I believe that speaking in tongues is a power gift. It is associated with warfare.

Paul says starting in Ephesians 6:10

> *Finally, be strong in the Lord*
> *and in the strength of His might.*
> *Put on the full armor of God,*
> *that you will be able to stand*
> *firm against the schemes of the devil.*
> *For our struggle is not against flesh and blood,*
> *but against the rulers, against the powers,*
> *against the world forces of this darkness,*
> *against the spiritual forces of wickedness*
> *in the heavenly places.*
> *Therefore, take on the full armor of God,*
> *so that you will be able to resist in the evil day,*
> *having done everything to stand.*
> *Stand firm therefore,*
> *having girded your loins with truth,*
> *and having put on the breastplate of righteousness,*
> *and having shod your feet with*
> *the preparation of the gospel of peace;*

in addition to all, take up the shield of faith
with which you will be able
to extinguish all the flaming arrows of the evil one.
And take the helmet of salvation,
<u>and the sword of the spirit,</u>
<u>which is the word of God.</u>
<u>With all prayer and petition pray</u>
<u>at all times in the Spirit</u>
and with this in view,
be on alert with all
perseverance and petition
for all the saints and pray on my behalf,
that utterance may be given to me
in the opening of my mouth,
to make known with boldness
the mystery of the gospel,
for which I am an ambassador in chains;
that in proclaiming it I may speak boldly,
as I ought to speak.

So, according to Paul, we are to *pray at all times in the Spirit!*

I can tell you from personal experience, that praying in the Spirit has brought about revelation, words of knowledge, and prophecy, and enhanced my prayer life immeasurably. Many serious Christian believers I know actively speak and pray in tongues. These people are not Sunday only Christians but live a laid down life.

I don't expect this information to end the long debate over tongues. I do suggest praying, studying, and proceeding as the Lord leads. Below is some information I found that is a summary of testing done concerning tongues. It is not comprehensive and using objective data to measure the supernatural is only an attempt to understand the phenomena.

Dr. Andrew Newborn from the University of Pennsylvania conducted a study in May of 2009 by scanning the brains of those speaking in tongues and then compared it to them praying, but in their known language. It appears that when praying in their native tongue, their frontal lobe was active. However, when scanning the brain of that same person speaking in tongues, their frontal lobe had a lower activity level.

His conclusion: Tongues is a more passive language, and although nothing can prove it is the Holy Spirit, it seems to confirm reports that speaking in tongues is different from other forms of communication.

Dr. Newborn repeated the same study on Buddhist monks and Franciscan nuns. Both scans were active when the language was engaging in native language prayer. This appeared on Nightline and heard on "All things Considered - Prayer May Reshape your Brain...And Your Reality" first broadcast May 20, 2009- third of a five part NPR series.

Then in June of 2011, Dr. Carl Peterson M.D. conducted

a study at Oral Roberts University in Tulsa, Oklahoma. He listed some health benefits of speaking in tongues. He said "Being a brain specialist, he was doing research on the relationship between the brain and praying or speaking in tongues. He found that as we pray in the Spirit or worship in the Spirit (our Heavenly language), the brain releases two chemical secretions that are directed into our immune system giving a 35 to 40 percent boost to the immune system. This promotes healing within our bodies. Amazingly, this secretion is triggered from a part of the brain that has no other apparent activity in humans and is only activated by our Spirit-led prayer and worship!

While these studies can never prove a supernatural experience, they certainly have an unexplainable outcome. But isn't that supernatural?

Prayer Scriptures Verses

John 15:7-8 "If you abide in Me, and My words abide in you, ask whatever you wish, and it will be done for you. My Father is glorified by this, that you bear much fruit, and so prove to be my disciples."

Mark 11:24 "Therefore I say to you, all things for which you pray and ask, believe that you have received them, and they will be granted you."

Romans 8:26 "In the same way the Spirit also helps our weakness: for we do not know how to pray as we should, but the Spirit Himself intercedes for us with groanings too deep for words; and He who searches the hearts knows what the mind of the Spirit is, because He intercedes for the saints according to the will of God."

Matthew 6:6-7 "But you, when you pray, go into your inner room, close your door and pray to your Father who is in secret, and your Father who sees what is done in secret will reward you. And when you are praying, do not use meaningless repetitions as the Gentiles do, for they suppose that they will be heard for their many words."

Luke 11:9 "So I say to you, ask, and it will be given to you; seek, and you will find; knock, and it will be opened to you."

Jeremiah 33:3 "Call to me and I will answer you, and I will tell you great and mighty things, which you do not know."

James 5:16 "Therefore, confess your sins to one another, and pray for one another so that you may be healed. The effective prayer of a righteous man can accomplish much."

1 Timothy 2:1-6 "First of all, then I urge that all supplications, prayers, intercessions, and thanksgivings, be made for all men, for kings and all who are in authority, so that we may lead a tranquil and quiet life in all godliness and dignity. This is good, and acceptable in the sight of God our Savior, who desires all men to be saved and come to the knowledge of the truth. For there is one God, and one mediator also between God and men, the man Christ Jesus, who gave Himself as a ransom for all, the testimony given at the proper time."

Matthew 26:41 "Keep watching and praying that you may not enter into temptation; the spirit is willing, but the flesh is weak."

Ephesians 6:18 "With all prayer and petition pray at all times in the Spirit, and with this in view be on the alert with all perseverance and petition for the Saints."

Psalm 34:17 "The righteous cry, and the Lord hears and delivers them out of troubles."

1 Timothy 2:8 "Therefore I want the men in every place to pray, lifting up holy hands, without wrath and dissension."

James 5:13-15 "Is anyone among you suffering? Then he must pray. Is anyone cheerful? He is to sing praises. Is anyone among you sick? Then he must call for the elders of the church, and let them pray for him, anointing him with oil in the name of the Lord; and the prayers of the faith will restore the one who is sick, and the Lord will raise him up, and if he has committed sins, they will be forgiven him.'

Matthew 18:19-20 "Again I say to you, if two of you agree on earth about anything they ask, it will be done for them by my father in heaven. For where two or three are gathered in my name, I am in their midst."

1 John 5:14–15 "This is the confidence which we had before Him, that, if we ask anything according to His will, He hears us. And if we know that He hears us in whatever we ask, we know that we have the request which we have asked from Him."

2 Chronicles 7:14 "If my people who are called by my name humble themselves, and pray and seek my face and turn from their wicked ways, then I will hear from heaven, and I will forgive their sins and heal their land."

PART 2

PRAISE

Ephesians 1:6

Let us praise God
For His glorious grace,
For the free gift He gave us
in His dear Son!

Isaiah 63:7

I will tell of the LORD's unfailing love;
I will praise Him for all He has done for us. He has richly
blessed the people of Israel because of His mercy and
constant love.

Why Praise?

I think a definition is a great place to start. Many will see the word praise and think singing, and rightly so. Praise is a form of singing and worship. But praise is so much more.

Praise: to express a favorable judgment of: commend

To glorify (a God or saint) especially by the attribution of perfections.

With that definition in mind, let's look at the well known Matthew 25 parable to see how and why an accurate and favorable judgment of God is so important.

 When we think of judgment, oftentimes it is us hoping to hear a favorable opinion from God of "well done good and faithful servant". The Bible states very clearly in Matthew 25 with the parable of the talents that, despite God being loving and kind, many have and do see him in a VERY different light.

Starting in verse 14:

"For it is just like the man about to go on a journey,
who called his own slaves,
and entrusted his possessions to them.
To one he gave five talents,
to another, two, and to another, one,
each according to his own ability;
and he went on his journey.

Immediately the one who had received the five talents
went and traded with them,
and gained five more talents.
In the same manner the one who had received the two
talents gained two more.
But he who received the one talent went away
and dug in the ground, and hid his masters money.
Now after a long time the master of those slaves came
and settled accounts with them.

And the one who had received the five talents came up
and brought five more talents, saying
'Master, you entrusted five talents to me;
see, I had gained five more talents'.
His master said to him,
'Well done, good and faithful slave;
you were faithful with a few things,
I will put you in charge of many things,
enter into the joy of your master.'

Also the one who had received two talents came up and
said, 'Master, you have entrusted to me two talents;
see, I had gained two more talents.'
His master said to him,
'Well done good and faithful slave;
you were faithful with a few things,
I will put you in charge of many things;
Enter into the joy of your master.'

And the one also who had received the one talent
came up and said 'Master,
'I knew you to be a hard man,
reaping where you did not sow
and gathering where you scattered no seed.
And I was afraid, and went away
and hid your talent in the ground.
See, you have what is yours.'

But his master answered and said to him,
'You wicked, lazy slave,
you knew that I reap where I did not sow,
and gather where I scattered no seed.
Then you ought to have put my money in the bank, and
upon arrival I would have received my money back with
interest.
Therefore take away the talent from him,
and give it to the one who has the ten talents.

For to everyone who has, more shall be given,
and he will have an abundance;
but from the one who does not have,
even what he does have shall be taken away.
Throw out the worthless slave into the outer darkness;
in that place there shall be weeping and gnashing of
teeth.''

So what does this parable have to do with praise?

EVERYTHING!

Consider for a moment this parable has nothing to do with money but instead it means talent or gifting. Certainly we could understand it to be anything God gives us. But even more importantly it has to do with *our* perception of God.

I myself had a false image and perception of who God is, just like the slave with the one talent. I feared God, and not in a biblical way with reverential awe, but I saw Him as a harsh, hard-handed, and a mean God who was impossible to please. Like I stated earlier, who can be perfect?

This parable is talking about money, but God is not concerned about what we earn. He is concerned about our heart and how *His children perceive Him.* We need to appreciate Him. We need to be good stewards of what we have been given certainly, but God cares more about our relationship with Him.

Think about this. Does God want us to double our interest or double His Kingdom taking the Gospel to the lost? God is neither poor nor greedy. He doesn't need our money. He wants us to share His love and Good News! This parable isn't about who God is; it is about how wrongly He is perceived! It was Satan's deception in the Garden and one he is still using today.

Our Father wants to lavish good things on His children, and again, this parable is not money, but how God's character is viewed. His abundance is about family, community, sharing the life we have with others and living life in healthy and joyful relationships. And look at how God addresses the slave who did not use his talents for good or to advance His Kingdom. He calls him a wicked servant.

If God gives us things to use to grow his Kingdom, things like prayer and prophecy, and we do not use them accordingly, will then God look upon that person as wicked? Again, translation matters.

Let's look at the Greek word used for wicked. It is *poneros*. It means hurtful and thus differing from essential character traits. The Lord is saying if you wrongly view Him as harsh, that it is hurtful. You do not have an accurate assessment of God, but rather you believe what you have *heard ABOUT* Him. We can essentially have a differing view of God that is *FLAWED* and it can significantly affect how we view Him and act towards Him and others!

This is in agreement with the other descriptive word used to describe the servant. Lazy. It is hurtful and grieving to not view God as the loving provider that He is. After all, He is the one who gave us *His talents* to begin with. We literally started with nothing!

One way to show someone that you are appreciative of them is to have a good and kind opinion of them, especially if it is deserved. And, if we go back to talents for a minute and view them as gifts (whether money or gifts of the Holy Spirit), isn't using them for Kingdom building honoring the person that gave them to you? Especially if we understand that using our gifts are not for us but others!

The gifts that we are given are earthly tools that we use here. They are not to be taken with us when we enter Heaven. However, what we do take with us are the souls of those that we have lived with, witnessed two, aided, taught, prayed for, prophesied to, and even given clothing, food or a small glass of water for Christ's sake.

I ask you to strongly consider looking at this parable again with fresh eyes. Are you using your gifts and talents for God's Kingdom?

Remember, the Holy Spirit IS GOD! He is an equal part of the Trinity. I feel He is often over looked or not considered. He is the GIVER of Gifts. In fact, it is He who decides what gift we receive. When you scoff at a gift, you scoff at the giver of the gift. We don't react negatively to the fruit of the Spirit, although we may neglect seeking them. Paul tells us to desire the gifts.

Do you have a gift of writing?

Do you have a talent for singing?

Have you been given the power to make money?

Are you a teacher or good with children?

Are you good with administration?

You won't need a spiritual test to know the answers to these questions. Just ask yourself what you have been complimented on. (Not that I am against a spiritual gifts test and think they may be beneficial).

What are you good at and what do you enjoy? God gives us the desires of our heart, and by that, I mean God puts them in our heart in the first place, so he wants us to live them out.

On another note, the Bible says that our heart can be wicked above all things and deceived so if you have it in your heart to commit robbery, adultery, or anything of that sort, it is NOT FROM YOUR HEAVENLY FATHER! Your heart needs to agree with His Word. That's why it is imperative you know it.

Perhaps playing music or art is your gifting.

Maybe you want to take a trip and be a missionary.

Ask for wisdom and provision.

Or you may be challenged to do something that you never desired or have no training in. If so and it is from the Lord, go for it. You may be miraculously endowed by the gift Giver. Don't be afraid of mistakes. We all make them and you will know soon enough either though confirmation or closed doors if it is not an area to pursue.

Please also note that dreams are often placed in our hearts many years before they become an actuality. Don't expect an instantaneous turn around when you have a thought, or desire, passion or calling. Seek the Lord, pray, and get direction from those mature believers around you and the wise and elders of your Church. God may need time to prepare you for what He is commissioning you to do. Remember, the bigger the calling, the bigger the prep time may be. Patience is a must.

Also, God moves us and introduces us to people who are part of our journey. Some of them walk with us for a short time, others for a greater length. It is all about growing in your talents (gifting) and calling. Please, do not despise small beginnings.

Using your gifts is essential or they would not have been given to you. God does not do things randomly. Your gifts are need for such a time as this.

In order to use your gifts correctly and to know what they are, you need to accurately understand Scripture. If you get tripped up on something, consider a Bible with the original languages or Word Study Bible and Dictionary. Hopefully, by now you understand why.

All the gifts, talents, and money in the world won't be of

use to you if you don't have a *good and accurate Biblical understanding of who God is.*

And since we are talking about praise, I will quote an all-time favorite worship song entitled, "Good, Good Father." Fulfilling your mission and developing your gifts may take time and sacrifice, so it is of the utmost importance that you know who God is. It is easy to praise and follow a good, loving Father. If your understanding of God is flawed, your mission may be a short-lived trip. Even under the best of circumstances, a calling can be difficult. But if your theology is wrong and you see God as punitive, your desire to "answer His calling" will be quick, if not readily dismissed.

Struggles will come on your journey. Remember, as your world seems upside down from time to time, or full of turmoil and tribulation, to hold onto the truth of the Bible when it says "all good and perfect gifts come from above" because knowing God will get you through. It is the enemy that comes to steal, kill and destroy! He wants your life and attention away from God and onto him, or your troubles, or others. Never lose your praise!

The other purpose of praise is to bring glory to God. Satan despises when we praise and worship God.

Why? Because some believe he was the Praise and Worship Director of Heaven under the name Lucifer. But God had no grace for Him. When pride came rushing into Lucifer, who desired to be like God and

54

tried claiming God's adoration for himself, his name was changed to Satan (which means adversary), and he was expelled. Remember, God has no adversary. Satan, however, is our adversary.

Where exactly did Satan go? Earth.

Read ISAIAH 14 and EZEKIEL 28

I recently saw a teaching from Perry Stone on how Heaven lost its song when Lucifer fell.

He proposes that the angels and creatures that surround the throne still proclaim HOLY, HOLY, HOLY, and WORTHY IS THE LAMB, but there was no longer a song or choir director.

According to Scripture, David, a man after God's own heart and a type and shadow of Christ, is the one who re-established 24/7 worship. This is unlike anything that had been done in Israel's history, but it was always part of God's plan.

This information is from "A Brief History of 24/7 Prayer: The Tabernacle of David. The Davidic Order of Worship" It states:

David included: 288 prophetic singers and 4000 musicians "to make petitions and give thanks and praise to the Lord" day and night!

This information is from "A Brief History of 24/7 Prayer: The Tabernacle of David. The Davidic Order of

Worship" It states:

"Although the tabernacle was replaced by a Temple, The Davidic order of worship was embraced and reinstituted by seven subsequent leaders in the history of Israel and Judah. Each time this order of worship was reintroduced, *spiritual breakthrough, deliverance, and military victory followed"*.

Evidently, it pleased ABBA.

Perhaps this is our a battle plan for our victory as well!

Evangelist Perry Stone and Pastor Robert Morris both do a fantastic job teaching on how man was created to Praise God! We are Heaven's replacement for the lost choir director.

Consider for a moment that we are made to praise and worship and how it affects all three parts of our being.

Our physical self participates by clapping, singing, and raising our hands or dancing. Our soulish realm partakes with joy, gratitude and healing. And, our spirit can connect with God and often we can, and do, receive words of knowledge, wisdom, prophecies, or even visions.

I would recommend either of these teachings by Perry Stone or Robert Morris and I would add Isaac Pitre's teaching on Divine DNA to top off a better understanding of who we are in Christ and who God intended us to be.

The book of Joshua provides yet another vital understanding, when we consider who and how we view God. This account from the 5th Chapter shows what happens to us when we align ourselves with *who* God is and *what* God is doing. We begin to understand the revelation that we have to stop trying to get God on our side and realize we need to be on His!

In Joshua 5:13-6:5, we read:

"Now it came about when Joshua was by Jericho,
that he lifted up his eyes and looked,
and behold, a man was standing opposite him
with his sword drawn in his hand,
and Joshua went to him and said to him,
'Are you for us or for our adversaries?'
He said, 'No; rather I indeed come now
as the Captain of the host of the Lord.'

And Joshua fell on his face to the earth,
and bowed down, and said to him,
'What has my Lord to say to his servant?'
The captain of the Lord's host said to Joshua
'Remove your sandals from your feet,
for the place where you are standing is holy.'
And Joshua did so.

Now Jericho was tightly shut because of the sons of

Israel: no one went out and no one came in. The Lord
said to Joshua,
'See, I have given Jericho into your hand,
with its king and the Valiant warriors.
You shall march around the city,
all the men of war circling the city once.
You shall do so for six days.
Also seven priests shall carry seven trumpets
of ram's horns before the Ark;
then on the seventh day
you shall march around the city seven times,
and the priest shall blow the trumpets.
It shall be that when they make a long blast
with the ram's horn,
and when you hear the sound of the trumpet,
all the people shall shout with s great shout;
and the wall of the city will fall down flat,
and the people Will go up every man straight ahead.'"

As Joshua did, so should we. He fell on his face to praise
and worship God, as should we fall on our face before
Our Lord! Victory is ours when we listen and obey.
Praise brought the people of God their victory! The
battle was won by using Heavenly warfare against an
earthly army.

God is a supreme being and worthy of all of our praises.
He deserves our best. He gave us HIS best, and He

deserves nothing less from us. Praise is what gets us to see Him high and lifted up. Praise doesn't bring God down but raises us up to Him. It can take us to Heavenly realms.

In the New Testament, 2 Corinthians 12:2, Paul writes:

"I know a man in Christ who fourteen years ago — whether in the body I do not know, or out of the body, God knows-such a man was caught up to the third heaven."

We know that God revealed mysteries to Paul. God is not a respecter of persons. What He did for Paul, He can do for us. And praise helps us see things from His perspective, both in the natural and the Heavenlies. When we see His perspective, it frees us from earthly challenges, worries, conflicts, and attachments. We are free to see and understand who we really are — sons-not slaves. Freedom is a great place to live.

In worship and praise, a hardened heart can be softened, hate can melt away, desires can change, and chains can break. I know. I have received that change.

At Freedom Community Church in Shrewsbury, PA, there were 21 days of fasting and prayer at the beginning of January 2019. During this time, remarkable things were happening.

On one particular rainy Thursday during the time of corporate prayer and praise at church, something happened. As the prayer and praise continued into the afternoon, the rain stopped, and suddenly we had beautiful sunshine cascading into the building. It felt like a reprieve of rain and I wanted to go outside thinking I might see a rainbow.

I went out but no rainbow. There was however something even more impressive waiting for me. I looked south and could see the nasty rain clouds still lingering so I began to scan to the west, north, east and back south again. I did a complete 360-degree turn. The Church was surrounded by dark rain clouds. It wasn't a front that was coming through but a literal circle of storm clouds except for a brilliant center of the sun shining down upon us. It was breathtaking and surreal all at the same time.

I have said for years that what we see happening in the physical is a sign as to what is happening in the spiritual. (Jesus cursing the fig tree, Matthew 21:18-22)

Another thing about praise is it changes our mind. As we praise we see things from a place of victory. Our victory is in Christ seated on His Throne.

Praise Scripture Verses

1 Chronicles 16:23-31 "Sing to the Lord, all the earth; Proclaim good tidings of His salvation from day to day. Tell of His glory among the nations, His wonderful deeds among all the peoples. For great is the Lord, and greatly to be praised; He also is to be feared above all gods. For all the gods of the peoples are idols, but the Lord made the heavens. Splendor and majesty are before Him, Strength and joy are in His place. Ascribe to the Lord, O families of the peoples, Ascribe to the Lord glory and strength. Ascribe to the Lord the glory due his name; Bring an offering and come before Him; Worship the Lord in holy array. Tremble before Him, all of the earth; Indeed, the world is firmly established, it will not be moved. Let the heavens be glad and let the earth rejoice; and let them say among the nations 'The Lord reigns'."

Daniel 2:20 "Let the name of God be blessed forever and ever, for wisdom and power belong to Him."

Deuteronomy 10:21 "He is your praise and He is your God, who has done great and awesome things for you which your eyes have seen."

Jeremiah 20:13 "Sing to the Lord, praise the Lord! For he has delivered the soul of the needy one from the hands of the evildoers."

Psalm 75:1 "We give thanks to you, O God, we give thanks, for Your name is near; Men declare your wondrous works."

Romans 12:1-2 "Therefore I urge you, brethren, by the mercies of God, to present your bodies a living and holy sacrifice, acceptable to God, which is your spiritual service of worship. And do not be conformed to this world, but be transformed by the renewing of your mind, so that you may prove what the will of God is, that which is good and acceptable and perfect."

Revelation 4:8-11 "And for living creatures, each one of them having six wings, are full of eyes around and within; and day and night they do not cease to say,
    'HOLY, HOLY, HOLY, is THE LORD GOD, THE ALMIGHTY, WHO WAS AND WHO IS AND WHO IS TO COME.'
    And when the living creatures give glory and honor and thanks to Him who sits on the throne, to Him who lives forever and ever, the twenty-four elders will fall down before Him who sits on the throne, and will worship Him who lives forever and ever, and will cast their crowns before the throne, saying,

"Worthy are you, our Lord and our God, to receive glory and honor and power; for you created all things, and because of your will they existed and were created."

Isaiah 29:13-14 "Then the Lord said, 'Because this people draw near me with their words And honor Me with their lip service, But they remove their hearts far from Me, and their reverence for Me consist of tradition learned by rote, Therefore behold, I will once again deal marvelously with these people, wondrously marvelous; And the wisdom of their wise men will perish, And the discernment of their discerning men will be concealed."

Hebrews 12:28 "Therefore, since we received a kingdom which cannot be shaken, let us show gratitude, by which we make an offer to God an acceptable service with reverence and awe; for our God is a consuming fire."

Psalm 100 "Shout joyfully to the Lord, all the earth. Serve the Lord with gladness; Come before Him with joyful singing. Know that the Lord himself is God; It is He who has made us, and not we ourselves; We are His people and the sheep of his pasture. Enter His gates with thanksgiving And his courts with praise. Give thanks to Him, bless His name. For the Lord is good; His lovingkindness is everlasting and His faithfulness to all generations."

PART 3

PROPHECY

Revelation 19:10

"Then I fell at his feet to worship him.
But he said to me, 'Do not do that;
I am a fellow servant of yours
and your brethren who hold
the testimony of Jesus;
worship God.
For the testimony of Jesus
is the spirit of prophecy'."

I want to begin this section by saying as New Covenant believers we live in a time that was declared a MYSTERY to the Jewish people living under the Old Covenant. We are fortunate enough to live in a time that the people of God longed for.

In Matthew 13:16-17, Jesus said to his disciples:

> "But blessed are your eyes,
> because they see;
> and your ears, because they hear.
> For truly I say to you that many prophets
> and righteous men desired to see
> what you see,
> and did not see it,
> and hear what you hear,
> and did not hear it."

We are told throughout the Old Testament that the Holy Spirit would COME upon His people. We live in a time when the Holy Spirit LIVES IN His people, and HE comes with the promise of never leaving us! And to be sure of that promise I will list several verses at the end of Part 3, both from the Old and New Testaments to confirm His promise.

It is also important to understand that our fellow Jewish Believers in Christ tend to look at prophecy differently. They view prophecy as a memorial to the past and a future fulfillment. Many in the modern church are unaware of the cyclical patterns in Scripture.

For instance, the Seven Feasts of Israel are to be celebrated both as a memorial AND a PROPHECY. It is a memorial to the goodness, faithfulness, and power of God as He delivered the Nation of Israel from Egypt. But, it is also a prophetic sign to the fulfillment of Yeshua's advent as their coming Messiah. Confusion may set in because Jesus fulfilled the first three Feasts when He first came as a man to die in our place. As our Passover Lamb He suffered and died. He was then buried as Unleavened bread, and resurrected during First Fruits as He became the first raised from the dead.

Pentecost, the forth Feast, occurring 50 days after First Fruits (Resurrection Sunday), was also fulfilled when the Holy Spirit came to the faithful 120 who stayed in Jerusalem waiting on the promise of Jesus.

The beautiful result of their obedience is not only did Pentecost fulfill the prophecy in Joel 2 that day, but through the Holy Spirit the 120 followers spoke in tongues and 3000 were saved.

Both the Church and Messianic believers are waiting for the fulfillment of the last 3 Fall feasts.

Jonathan Cahn, a Jewish Rabbi, has several books on this subject which is fascinating and can explain in detail prophetic patterns and cycles in the Hebrew writings.

As you can see, prophecy can reveal itself in different ways but it's important we understand prophecy. These definitions are from "The Prophet's Dictionary" by Dr. Paula A. Price Ph.D.

According to Dr. Price, prophecy is the inspiration to declare, tell forth, or reveal the word of the Lord. It is the act of predicting the future as inspired by the anointing of the Lord.[1]

Often prophecy is confused with a word of knowledge which is one of the nine manifestations of the gifts of the Holy Spirit that we see in 1 Corinthians 12.

According to Dr. Price, a word of knowledge: is delivered by the Spirit of God supernaturally. Words of knowledge manifestations are usually short, often single word sentences that provide information for the hearer to act on while being used of God.

Dr. Price says for clarity, the term found in 1 Corinthians 12:8 would be understood as the "statement of knowledge, more of fact" for that is how it emerges to the hearer.[2]

Now, let's look at covenants.

Today when we prepare an estate and consider leaving our children an inheritance, we go to a lawyer (or an online service) and make out a will. When I was a child, I remember distinctly hearing about relatives passing and

---

[1] Paula A Price, *The Prophet's Dictionary* (New Kensington, PA: Whitaker House, 1999), p. 399
[2] Ibid. p. 593

reading their last will and testament.

Today the verbiage "will and testament" is lost from our understanding because it's lost from our vocabulary.

Traditionally upon the death of someone, their last will and testament can list very specific instructions on how, what, and when things are to be carried out. It may include what will happen to the remains of the deceased, what will happen to property, clothing, jewelry, asset, etc. Any of this sounding familiar to you?

With that, think of the Old Testament as instructions to the CHILDREN of Israel. They were called children in the Old Testament and for the most part, treated as such under the Law. They had very specific instructions on how to carry out the sacrifices and stringent penalties for failing to do so, as well as severe consequences when they failed to obey the Law.

Their government was administered by Judges first, then Kings, Priests, and of course, Prophets.

The King was an overseer to the people as a guardian. He was to rule wisely and represent the Kingdom of Israel as the Chosen people before the world and cause a jealously so that the world would see and understand God and long to be a part of His Kingdom here on Earth.

The High Priest represented *the people before God.* He offered sacrifices so that the people's sins would be

COVERED and they would be acceptable to a Holy God.

The Prophet *represented God to the people*. He would hear from God and instruct them on the condition of their standing with God and offer instructions, warnings, and hope to and for the people.

And all this became necessary because of a sin committed in the Garden of Eden by Adam and Eve.

We read in Genesis that Adam and Eve were put here on earth to rule and reign (Kingship). They were caretakers, administrators, and they walked and talked with God and even had the authority to name the animals which is the role of Prophets. Another role of Prophets is to call out sin and direct the people back to God. The Priesthood was necessary because of the sin committed by Adam and Eve. Prior to the original sin, the sacrifice and priesthood was not necessary.

They were living Kingdom lives along with God-until they weren't. One act of disobedience changed the trajectory of all mankind. But God did not leave us to our own demise. He set up a shadow kingdom until a time when man could rule again. I use the term shadow because that is how the Bible refers to it.

Hebrews 7:26-8:5 says,

"For it was fitting for us to have such a High Priest,
holy, innocent, undefiled, separated from sinners and
exalted above the heavens;
who does not need daily,
like those high priests,
to offer up sacrifices, first for his sins,
and then for the sins of the people,
because this He did once for all
when He offered up Himself.
For the law appoints men as high priests who are weak,
but the word of the oath,
which came after the law,
appoints a Son,
made perfect forever.

Now the main point in what has been said is this;
we have such a high priest,
who has taken His seat at the right hand of the throne
of the Majesty in the heavens,
a minister in the sanctuary,
and in the true tabernacle,
which the Lord pitched, not man.
For every high priest is appointed to offer
both gifts and sacrifices;
So it is necessary,
that this high priest
also have something to offer.

Now if He were on earth,
He would not be a priest at all,
since there are those who offer the gifts
according to the Law;
who serve a copy and a shadow
of the heavenly things,
just as Moses was warned by God
when he was about to erect the tabernacle;
for, 'See, He says,
THAT YOU MAKE all things
ACCORDING TO THE PATTERN WHICH WAS SHOWN
YOU ON THE MOUNTAIN'.
But now He has obtained a
more excellent ministry,
by as much as He is also
the mediator
of a better covenant,
which has been enacted
on better promises."

Despite many sins and much disobedience along the way God's plan would come in the fullness of time.

Galatians 4:4-7

"But when the fullness of time had come,
God sent forth his Son,
Born of woman, born under the Law,
so that He might redeem those who were under the

Law, that we might receive adoption as sons.

Because you are sons,
God has sent a Spirit of His Son
into our hearts,
crying Abba! Father!
so you are no longer a slave
but a son, and if a son,
then an heir through God."

He found a few faithful in a world that wasn't interested in Him or His plan. See Hebrews Chapter 11, often referred to as the Hall of Faith!

Eventually, a will (Old Testament) was set up to leave the children (Israel) with a way to be taken care of and instructions on how to represent the King, and most importantly, WHEN the contract would be completed and by WHOM!

This New contract (New Will and Testament) gave us rights and responsibilities, only now as adults.
See 1 John.

We no longer need an overseer and administrator (King and Priests). We are told we are Kings and Priests (note that currently Jesus is our High Priest who sits at the right hand of the Father and makes intercession for us continually until He comes back for His Bride).

We all have gifts given to us by the Holy Spirit at our salvation to use for Kingdom purposes. And one of those gifts is the ability to hear GOD'S VOICE! And while I believe we still have prophets among us, every one of us can hear from God!

Let's look at John 10:1-18.

"Truly, truly, I say to you,
he who does not enter by the door
into the fold of the sheep,
but climbs up some other way,
he is a thief and a robber.
But he who enters the door is a shepherd
of the sheep.
To him the doorkeeper opens,
and the sheep hear his voice,
and he calls his sheep by name
and leads them out.
When he puts forth all his own, he goes ahead
of them, and the sheep follow him
because they know his voice.
A stranger they will not follow,
but will flee from him,
because they do not know the voice of strangers."

This figure of speech Jesus spoke to them,
but they did not understand what those things were
which He had been saying to them.

So Jesus said to them again,

"Truly, truly, I say to you I am the door of the sheep.
All who came before me are thieves and robbers, but the
sheep did not hear them.
I am in the door: if anyone enters through Me,
He will be saved, and shall go in and out and find
pasture. The thief comes only to steal and kill and
destroy; I come they may have life,
and have it abundantly.

I am the good shepherd;
the good Shepherd lays down his life
for the sheep.
He who is a hired hand,
and not a shepherd,
who is not the owner of the sheep,
sees the wolf coming,
and leaves the sheep and flees,
and the Wolf snatches them.
He flees because he is a hired hand
and is not concerned about the sheep.

I am the good Shepherd,
and I know My own and my own know me,
even as the Father knows me and I know the Father:
and I lay down my life for the sheep.
I have other sheep, which or not of this fold;

I must bring them in also and they will hear my voice,
and they will become one flock with one Shepherd.
For this reason, the Father loves Me,
because I laid down My life so that I may take it again.
No one has taken it away from me,
but I lay it down of my own initiative.
I have authority to lay it down,
and I have authority to take it up again.
This commandment I received from My Father."

It is clear, as God's children and family, we can hear His voice. The Bible wants us to see ourselves as children because God wants us to understand the premise of adoption. We are adopted - grafted in, to His family under the new covenant or testament. But God wants our relationship to go so much further. He wants to call us his friend. And more importantly, God wants us to be part of his plan!

Speaking of God's prophetic plan…I want to mention a very important concept that Christian author and speaker, John Bevere talks about in his book "The Fear of The Lord." If you are like me, you may wonder why God's judgments are sometimes swift and sure while other times they are long-awaited and delayed. Thankfully, John Bevere explains this perfectly and it has to do with prophecy!

He writes, "Compare the sin of Eli's sons, with the sin of

Aaron's sons, Nadab and Abihu (the man who died when they brought profane fire before the Lord). It is hard to avoid questioning why Eli's sons were not judged with death just as quickly. Their sin was blatant, total disrespect for God, His people, and His offerings. Why, then, were they not judged the same–with immediate death at the tabernacle."[3]

Our answer is found in the following verse:

> **1 Samuel 3: 1-3 "The <u>word of the Lord was rare</u> in those days; there was no widespread revelation. And it came to pass at that time, while Eli was lying down in his place, and when his eyes had begun to grow dim that he could not see, and before the lamb of God went out in the tabernacle of the Lord where the ark of God was..."**

Bevere goes on to show us four points in his book:

1) The word of the Lord was rare (*prophecy*).

2) There was no widespread revelation (*wisdom and knowledge*).

3) The eyes of leadership were darkened that they could not see (*Spiritually blinded*).

4) The lamp of God was going out."

---

[3] John Bevere, *The Fear of the Lord* (Lake Mary, FL: Charisma House, 1997), p. 90.

We as a church, especially in America, have been spared Judgment because prophecy and revelation have been scarce. They have been scarce because many in the church do not believe they are still relevant or even desire them. Many, especially Pastors, are blind to the truth of prophecy or choose not to teach on the gifts. I believe that those who do not come into agreement with God's word will soon not have a platform.

Time is short, and God is ready to share His heart and His Faith, and His Spirit with ALL His people, not just a few. The harvest is ripe, but the workers have been few.

Until NOW!

Prophecy and revelation are growing. Words of Knowledge are abounding. His Church is once again having a resurgence of the gifts, ALL THE GIFTS! But, caution is needed. Not everyone who claims to be a prophet is a prophet. They may think they are, but caution is always needed. Words of Knowledge and Prophecies must always agree with Holy Scripture.

Not every word of knowledge or prophecy is indeed from God. There are false prophets sent to destroy the Church. God warns us all *to tests the spirits*. That can only be done by knowing the WORD of God. And remember, God will confirm His Word! So, after any sermon or conference, it is essential to check the pastor's or speaker's information to see if what he is saying lines up with God's Word.

Another issue is that a word or prophecy may be wrongly interpreted, leading astray those who received it. Beware, because with information comes responsibility and yes, even judgment!

Just in case you need more to convince you, consider these scripture verses about hearing from the LORD.

Genesis 18:17

> "The Lord said, 'Shall I hide from Abraham
> what I am about to do,
> since Abraham will surely become
> a great and mighty nation,
> and in him all the nations of the earth
> will be blessed'?"

Exodus 33:11

> "The Lord used to speak to Moses face to face,
> just as a man speaks to his friend."

Zechariah 13:6

> "And one will say to him,
> 'What are these wounds between your arms'?
> Then he will say, 'Those with which I was wounded in
> the house of my friends."

John 15:13

"Greater love has no one than this,
that one lay down his life for his friends.
You are My friends if you do what I command you. No
longer do I call you slaves,
for the slave does not know what his master is doing:
but I have called you friends,
for all things that I've heard from My Father
I had made known to you."

James 2:23

"And the scripture was fulfilled which says,
'and Abraham believed God,
and it was reckoned to him as righteousness,'
and he was called the friend of God."

I want to share one last thing about prophecy and its connection to dreams. While not every dream contains a prophecy, DREAMS can and do at times include messages for us, for others, and give insight that we need from God.

Dr. Price, in the Prophet's Dictionary defines a prophetic dream as,[4]

"A dream had by a prophet or by one who is not a prophet, indicative of a prophecy because of its

---

[4] Paula A Price, *The Prophet's Dictionary* (New Kensington, PA: Whitaker House, 1999), p. 418

predictive or revelatory implications. Prophetic dreams serve the distinct purpose of being divine and spiritual communication vehicles. [See Genesis 20:3]."

"Prophetic dreams impart visions, deposit God's words, or establish spiritual truth. They are often used as precursors to a move of God and confirm something He has just done in the spirit realm that has yet to appear in physical form."

"Prophetic dreams differ from prophetic visions in that the prophetic dreams, though predictive or revelatory in nature, is communicated in language and symbolism that is relevant to the dreamers' sphere of life. Metaphors and parables are delivered using images and vernacular the dreamer can relate to when proving the dream upon awakening."

"A prophetic dream, furthermore, is one in which, upon waking, the dreamer finds details vividly etched in his or her mind. The experience of the prophetic dreams means the Lord is implanting message in the dreamer's heart or mind. The familiar emblems of the dream may pertain to the dreamers' profession, cultural background or history, family tree, or life experience. Visions present themselves, although sometimes within a dream, in language and imagery that is independent of these. This holds true even if the subject matter of the dream is one to which the dreamer can relate. See also Job 33: 14-16"

Here is an example of a message delivered in a dream. It was a message of how and what to pray that can bring deliverance from fear, doubt, lack of experiencing healing and a change of mind to those who are in unbelief.

CJ's Dream

My daughter Cassandra Joy had a dream.
CJ, her sister Savannah, and several others were in a WHITE ROOM. She says most of her dreams are in white rooms. By the way, the color white is symbolic of victory, righteousness, and purity.

Four others accompanied her. In the dream, a young woman was having pains in her legs, and could not walk. Looking on was another friend, who does not believe that healings and miracles exist today. He was watching and waiting to see what the young ladies would do.

The girls decided to pray and declare healing to their injured friend. The onlooker was smirking because of his unbelief. He doubted, and was making it apparent to them. His unbelief and doubt shook the group, and they felt fear come into the white room.

CJ and the group began to pray. CJ then got a Word from the Lord. He told her to pray for *faith!* She began praying for faith, and the atmosphere in the room changed! As they declared Heaven's desire, the injured legs were healed!

Excitement and praise were filling the room.

CJ looked to her doubting Thomas friend, (not his name but I refer to the disciple who doubted) and he was shocked. He began to cry and shake. He was amazed! He could no longer say that healing was not for today. He saw it with his own eyes and began crying. He soon was filled with joy and repented of his doubt!

I was excited about this dream. I believe it to be prophetic right down to the room color! I pray for my daughters' friends, all of them, but especially for the unbelieving believers! The church is filled with unbelieving believers. That is why I believe God prompted me to write this book.

If you are reading this, you were prayed for too. We serve a supernatural God. He uses supernatural things to reach the unsaved and even his own who have been wrongly taught or blinded by the enemy's tactics.

All God's promises are yes and amen.

Read His word

Believe what you read!

Study to show yourself approved.

Prophecy Scripture Verses

Luke 1:70 "As he spoke by the mouth of his holy prophets from old…"

1 Corinthians 13:2 "If I have the gift of prophecy, and know all mysteries and all knowledge; and if I have all faith, so as to remove mountains, but do not have love, I am nothing."

2 Peter 1:21 "For no prophecy was ever made by an act of human will, but men moved by the Holy Spirit spoke from God."

1 John 4:1-3 "Beloved, do not believe every spirit, but test the spirits to see whether they are from God, because many false prophets have gone out into the world. By this you know the Spirit of God: every spirit that confesses that Jesus Christ has come in this flesh is from God, and every spirit that does not confess Jesus is not from God; this is the spirit of the antichrist, of which you have heard that is coming, and now it's already in the world."

Amos 3:7 "Surely the Lord God does nothing unless He reveals His secret counsel to His servants the prophets."

Ephesians 2:19-20 "So then you are no longer strangers and aliens, but you are fellow citizens with the saints, and are of God's household, having been built on the foundation of the apostles and prophets, Christ Jesus Himself being the cornerstone, in whom the whole building, being fitted together, is growing into a holy temple in the Lord, in whom you also are being built together into a dwelling of God in the Spirit."

Acts 19:5-6 "When he heard this, they were baptized in the name of the Lord Jesus. And when Paul had laid his hands upon them, the Holy Spirit came on them, and they began speaking with tongues and prophesying."

Matthew 1:19-20 "And Joseph her husband, being a righteous man and not wanting to disgrace her, planned to send her away secretly. But when he had considered this, behold, an angel of the Lord appeared to him in a dream, saying, "Joseph, son of David, do not be afraid to take Mary as your wife; for the child who has been conceived in her is of the Holy Spirit."

Joel 2:28 "It will come about after this that I will pour out My Spirit on all mankind, and your sons and daughters will prophesy, your old men will dream dreams, your young men will see visions. And even on the male and female servants I will pour out my Spirit in those days."

Old Testament Promises

Joshua 1:9 "Have I not commanded you? Be strong and courageous. Do not be frightened, and do not be dismayed, for the Lord your God is with you wherever you go."

Isaiah 41:10 "Fear not, for I am with you; be not dismayed, for I am your God; I will strengthen you, I will help you, I will uphold you with my righteous right hand."

Deuteronomy 31:6 "Be strong and courageous. Do not fear or be in dread of them, for it is the Lord your God who goes with you. He will not leave you or forsake you."

The reason I want to emphasize this point is that even under the Old covenant God was watching out for and caring for his people. Although access to God may have varied, the people of God were never away from God's heart, and we are told that Israel is the apple of God's eye [Zechariah 2:8].

New Testament Promises

Matthew 28:20 "Teaching them to observe all that I had commanded you. And behold, I am with you always, to the end of the age."

Hebrews 13:5 "Keep your life free from the love of money, and be content with what you have, for he has said, I will never leave you nor forsake you."

Romans 8:38-39 "For I am sure that neither death nor life, nor angels nor rulers, nor things present nor things to come, nor Powers, nor height nor depth, nor anything else in all creation, will be able to separate us from the love of God which is in Christ Jesus our Lord."

Conclusion

There may be some questions about what you have read here. One big question is "I have prayed for people. "Why didn't God answer my prayers?"

Please know, we are not God, and only God can answer our prayers. Only God heals. We pray and declare as we receive. We are NOT the ones healing or performing miracles - EVER! Our responsibility is to be faithful to our calling and leave the outcome to HIM! Sometimes He answers our prayers in ways we didn't expect.

Remember, some people may not want prayer. I have encountered them. Some may not want healing. They may be afraid of life without their impairment. Yes, they may be more fearful of living whole than what they have become accustomed to. Physical ailments are not different from emotional ailments. Some like to stay where they are. They may not want the pain or circumstances, but they choose that over the unknown. Some prefer to follow their idea of God rather than the God of the Bible (their perceived version).

I attended a prophecy conference in Lancaster, PA a few years ago, and I remember an account told by the Pastor who was presenting. He recalled driving with a friend (and fellow Pastor) when the Lord prompted them to stop at a particular house and ask if they could pray for someone with cancer. An older lady answered the door, and the men asked if someone was there that had cancer because God had sent them to pray for healing for them.

Indeed, there was a retired Pastor with cancer in that home. His wife acknowledged that her husband was there and he had cancer. When they asked if they could pray for him, her response was unexpected. Her husband was a Pastor, but she explained to the pair that they did not believe in healing, and she declined their offer to pray. I would like to think if a stranger came to my door and I had a similar experience that I would let them in.

What would you do?

Psalm 78:41 KJV
"Yea, they turn back and tempted God, AND LIMITED THE HOLY ONE OF ISRAEL."

This Scripture verse is referring to Israel as they traveled in the wilderness. In our wilderness and everywhere else we just need to be FAITHFUL!

ONE THING FOR CERTAIN, WE ALL NEED TO STOP LIMITING GOD!

"And after He had come into the house, the blind man
came to Him, and Jesus said to them,
Do you believe that I am able to do this?
They said to Him, "Yes Lord.
Then He touched their eyes, saying,
'Be it done to you according to your faith.'
And their eyes were opened."

May we believe and may our eyes be opened!

Another aspect of healing, especially for the elderly, or
chronically sick, is that they may choose death over the
suffering they are enduring. Some long to be reunited
with loved ones, or for the pain to stop, or they simply
lose the will to live. Often, they will not express this to
their loved ones who don't want to let go.

And sometimes, people need to be told that it is ok to
go…

When my Mom was suffering in the last few days of her
life, a doctor approached us as we were trying to figure
out where she should go. We were deciding between
home and hospice. When the doctor asked her where
she wanted to go, she weakly looked up at him and
simple said "Heaven." She went just hours later.

Just as an ending note, it is important for me to share
that this is not a *formula, a religious ritual,* or in any way
legalistic. Just the opposite. It is a key. It opens doors to

the Kingdom and things not possible without them.

This book is in no way comprehensive. It is meant as a springboard to dive further into these topics. It is to bring Scripture into a relevant context, introduce you to other Pastors and Authors, and whet your appetite for more.

It is doing God's work, God's way.

It is following in Jesus' footsteps.

I don't expect all who may read this book to agree with it, but I ask that you do your homework and pray and ask God just what He has in store for you. Ask Him for your key.

Romans 12:1 "Therefore I urge you, brethren, by the mercies of God, to present your bodies a living sacrifice, acceptable to God, which is your spiritual service of worship."

John 14:12 "Truly, truly, I say to you, he who believes in Me, the works that I do, he will do also; and greater works than these he will do; because I go to the Father."

Peace and Love to you.

About the Author

Kathy Hanson began working in the Health and Educational field after graduating from Towson State University. Her whole life began to change in her late twenties when she was introduced to a personal relationship with Jesus Christ. She later attended Baltimore School of the Bible and has had the pleasure to study the Bible as well as pray for and help others understand Scripture in both personal and group settings.

Made in the USA
Middletown, DE
29 June 2019